Simple ways to boost your beauty

By Jean Young

EXPERIENCE EVERYTHING
P U B L I S H I N G

Disclaimer

This document is geared towards providing exact and reliable information in regards to the topic and issue covered. The publication is sold with the idea that the publisher is not required to render accounting, officially permitted, or otherwise, qualified services. If advice is necessary, legal or professional, a practiced individual in the profession should be ordered.

- From a Declaration of Principles which was accepted and approved equally by a Committee of the American Bar Association and a Committee of Publishers and Associations:

The information herein is offered for informational purposes solely, and is universal as so. The presentation of the information is without contract or any type of guarantee assurance.

Introduction

"Beauty is in the eye of the beholder"

This is a very old proverb that is often said when people are challenged with the standards of beauty. Not everyone realized it, and they may have completely ignored it, but the standards of how beauty is perceived through the times have changed. If you have lived between the 1970s to 1980s decade, comparing the standards of beauty that time is totally different today, even if fashion has been rehashed or picked up again in modern times. Thanks to the influence of mass media, it has driven some people to achieve such standards to extreme levels that there are cases where cosmetic procedures have disfigured their physical appearance – all in the name of beauty.

You will be baffled with how beauty was seen in the decades past, especially if you look back hundreds of years ago. You might even mumble to yourself how you wish you live back in the past, but you don't want to be caught up in the middle of a war, right? Those times were quite harsh for people, so getting to understand who sets up the standards of beauty will give you the good idea that it is okay to follow your own standards of beauty.

History

Beauty is not only skin deep. It entirely depends on the time you have lived. In every time period in history, various ideas have emerged on how beauty is defined.

Paler Beauty

In the past, pale skin was often seen as the ultimate beauty. It didn't matter what kind of face or figure you had, as long as you had the pale skin that people were looking for. In history, having a tan skin meant that you have been working outside the whole day. This was an indication to the people that time you have been farming and therefore, lower class. If you display pale skin, this means that you cannot afford to be outside the whole time and have spending the rest of your day indoors. However, not all women are naturally pale, which is why they invented ways to make themselves look pale, even to the brink of absurdity that it costed them their lives – by faking a pale skin with the use of a titanium paint, which is proven to be poisonous to the human body. It was also the time "blue blood" became a popular term referring to the wealthy elite. Most of the women of this time wanted to be pale that bad that you will be able to see the blood veins on their face – they can either be natural or painted on the skin.

Perfume Bath of the Ancients

Although there are certain cultures today that prefer to have showers daily, it is sometimes on the last of your list to do in the morning. But when you include cultures like that of ancient India and Rome wherein the baths were considered social arenas, it is to be expected that bathing was an activity done during the seasons. This also means that they only get to bathe when needed.

But instead of using the usual soap and water, everyone in the bathhouses preferred to shower themselves with excessive amounts of perfume.

The Weighty and Curvy

Did you know that classic painting was supposed to be painting real life people? And in those paintings, some of them even have very weighty and curvy women? This was considered the standard of beauty in those times. It was also viewed as cool – during the times when food was very scarce that people barely had anything to eat, except in the past hundred years. Being fully figured, weighty and curvy means that you had enough food to eat and considered a potentially rich and healthy mate.

However, during the past century the emphasis placed upon mass consumption meant to the wealthy elite that they need to put a limit to their eating so that they get to stand out from the rest of the people, especially during the times when the middle class are starting to eat a lot. The skinnier people started to become fashionable, and it has been stuck in that standard for very long, even up to this day.

The Cool Wigs

There were times in history that get you wondered how women of the elite and wealthy class were able to come up with such elaborate hairstyles. It turns out that they were wearing wigs. Having long hair meant a status symbol to the public, particularly during the pre-hygenic societies. It was difficult that time to maintain long hair when they had only limited number to bathe themselves. It also signified that energy and time that only the wealthy elite can have.

During the 17th century, diseases acquired through sexual intercourse made it inside Europe's royal courts and often resulted baldness! They were not willing to give up their locks, which made them go on wearing wigs. The bigger wig they wore, the greater its cost, adding to it's purpose of being a status symbol.

Less Blonde

Being blonde these days often gets a good reputation, but they did not have that same attention back in the times when it was considered someone belonging to the barbaric North tribe. Blond hair was considered a social stigma, especially around the Roman Empire. Blonde was only considered fashionable in few hundred years in the past, especially that coming from one of the stunning paintings by Botticelli. It made the blonde colored hair the most sought after by women. It reached its peak around the 1950s decade where iconic women like Marilyn Monroe had platinum blonde hair.

The Red Hair

No matter what point in history you are going to look at, fiery ladies, or those with red hair has often been the most preferred color, whether they are natural or faked. The rarity of red hair makes it extra special. A person's ability in dyeing one's hair with any natural agents like henna that would produce a natural-looking red hair made it an elite activity practice in societies in the pre-Industrial times.

Cosmetics in the Ancients

Museums have a lot of make-up tools and palettes from the ancient past that most of the women during those times utilized in order to maintain their beauty. But since the ones displayed inside museums are aimed towards Mediterranean's ancient cultures, people these days are getting a distorted view of make-up's history.

Make-up wasn't actually that popular in the past. Using make-up was a sign that the woman was a prostitute or a "floozy". All over Europe, make-up did not get into trend up until the time when Queen Elizabeth I began to cover her face with white make-up. And even that time, there was only limited use of the whole face powder and paint. Anything other than that was considered rare and even scandalous.

The Rise of Modern Make-Up

It was only until many years have passed that make-up has become a standard for women, especially during the modern times. Thank technology for making make-up very accessible. This was becoming true when film industry began to emerge. In order not to look like their faces are washed out when cameras and lights were pointed at them, they began exaggerating their lips and eyes with make-up. Thus, the rest of the world followed.

The early films also set audiences in America onto a new pathway on how eyebrows are done. Prior to the makeover of eyebrows, it was left to nature on how it should be shaped. However, one particular iconic female launched the straight, thin brows and became a fashion mainstream in the 20th century. It did not last long though – around the 50s thick brows went back into popularity. In these days, almost any kind of eyebrow is acceptable.

Hair Shaving

There are records in history that showed shaving was common, but it was set on men athletes and not on women. What's more, it was only done on an occasional basis.

The current infatuations of modern society wherein armpits, arms and legs are shaved thoroughly is something that started in the early 20th century. It first started as changing the senses and hemlines of propriety on things about what women could wear and could not wear. Since the capitalists wanted more customers to buy their products, especially companies that sell shaving blades for men, they started advertising to women with regard to the benefits of shaving. In modern times, it has been ingrained into the psyche of women of how important it is to shave the armpits and legs, whether it is true or not.

Another recent trend is the full-scale removal of pubic hair. This is a modern approach which may have stemmed from the increased popularity of pornography. Brazilian wax was considered a scandalous movement when it first came out but because the increasing visibility of the human body on-screen, it became very popular.

The Intensity of Plastic Surgery

Plastic surgery was initially used in the medical field to fix people that are born with defects or those who had accidents that deformed their physical appearance. But behind these medical fixes, the wealthy and the movie stars started to patronize plastic surgeons for various superficial reasons. For decades, it was seen scandalous to have such work done on your body however even though plastic surgery started with a stigma on how inappropriate it is to change your natural physical appearance, it dissipated over time. This is thanks to the role that reality TV has played in mainstream media. The perceived ease in which the wealthy celebrities of particular shows have undertaken breast augmentations, Botox and nose jobs has encouraged the lower and middle class to follow suit.

Tiny Waists

Even before the advancements of medicine that made it possible to have plastic surgery, the one that was really popular during that time when undertaking the beautification process was mainly pointed around the waist of the lady. A tinier waist was viewed as better, even if they had to constantly bind themselves and break a rib or two just to get the mid-section of the body look smaller. Even though the whale bone corsets that were highly used during the Victorian period have fallen out of fashion, smaller waists seem to be more accepted, especially around the burlesque scene and through the use of "waist trainers" in mainstream western society.

Shoulder Pads

Back in the 1980s, especially in America, there was a particularly interesting fashion that is now considered tacky by modern experts. Amongst them was shoulder pads, big hair, overdone makeup, not to mention how fashion was done in a variety of bizarre ways. It clearly showed how the fashion industry was trying to mold all the beauty standards of the past and only lasted for a brief time.

Geeky Look

Intelligence, for the first time in history, is accepted as the prime key in what makes the people, both men and women, look beautiful and sexy. You can see a lot of people get obsessed with musicians, actors and actresses that have the nerdy look including stereotypical items such as large glasses and suspenders.

Section 1: Beauty Standards of the World

Before you make any philosophical claims about how beauty depends on each person's perspective, you have to learn that in every country or place you visit, they have their own standards of beauty. If you look at the standard of beauty in general, particularly in mainstream media, it focuses more on Caucasian women, although there are the occasional varieties, too. This has led to discussions regarding how mainstream media tends to objectify a specific skin color as their models, but these days, more and more, fashion runways also feature women from all over the world.

If you travel far and wide, you will realize that the old phrase mentioned in the introduction holds true. Beauty is truly in the eye of the beholder. As you watch various couples throughout your life, you must have realized at one point that there were pairs that did not seem to match up according to your standards of beauty. Women have done things to the extreme when it comes to beauty such as tanning beds, Brazilian waxes or eyelash extensions just to name a few. But as you get to meet different people and inquire about their opinion of beauty, you will realize that what you might have been doing to your body are totally crazy to their point of view. If you wish to know more about many definitions of beauty, you must travel around the world and look closely how each culture define beauty.

Body Scars
Generally, women all over the world are scared of having their skin scarred. However, if you travel to Ethiopia, you will be stunned at the fact that the women there deliberately make scars on their skin. The Karo tribe is fond of doing that to their own bodies. This is because the scar itself represent beauty and it means that it is literally deeper than skin. The scars are cut onto the women's stomachs at early childhood. These are considered adornments that is designed to attract men that are a potential husband.

Shaved Heads, Long Earlobes
From Ethiopia, your next destination should be at Kenya where you will get to meet the Masai tribe. Women in that tribe have stretched their earlobes to the point that it reaches the chest. Not only that, they also shave their heads, making it an ideal picture of a beautiful woman in their tribe. Women there are widely known for shaving their heads. They use almost everything they see such as twigs or elephant tusks in stretching and piercing their ear lobes, making it more attractive to men.

Long Necks

Jump your way to Thailand and meet the women in the Kayan tribe. You will see women there wearing heavy brass rings around their necks. To those who are not familiar with this kind of tradition, you will be surprised at the number of rings that are placed on top of one ring to the other. At an early age of five, women start adorning their necks with the brass rings. Every year, one coil is added on top, thus pushing their shoulders down and making an illusion of a longer neck. You might hear women who have undergone a medical procedure for beauty saying it is such a pain, but bear in mind that the Kayan women have been keeping this ritual for many centuries, not to mention that all rings can weigh for up to 22 pounds.

Pale Skin

Wasn't pale skin already mentioned in history, and how women were so desperate that they had to use a poisonous chemical just to achieve that pale skin in the past? But if you go to China, Japan and Thailand, pale skin is a natural color for them. Not only in these countries, but several parts of Asia revere white skin as a symbol of attractiveness and affluence. The women in Japan are known to avoid the sun at all costs, which is why they wear parasols a lot, even if they are not living in Japan. Skin care products are dominated with whitening agents, which is especially popular in Thailand, China and many other parts of Asia. Almost every skincare products in these parts have bleaching properties added to it.

Face Tattoos

The Maori tribe in New Zealand still exist today, and one of their sacred rituals performed exclusively for women is tattooing. Unlike in other cultures where tattooing the skin is considered rebellious and dirty, the people of the Maori tribe view this as a symbol of beauty, particularly with women. According to tradition, a chisel was utilized in carving grooves into their skin, although these days tattoo machines are mainly used. The design is more of swirls, referred to as Ta-molo. Women who bear tattooed chins and lips, plus full blue lips are considered amongst them as the most beautiful.

Full Figures
While the rest of the world has seen dieting as a way to achieve thinness, cultures in Western Africa find women that are overweight to be very gorgeous. The more these women have stretch marks, the better it will be for the eyes of their men. If you study about their past, it is not unheard of that the families in Mauritania would send their daughters to a camp referred to as "fat farms" wherein the girls are forced to eat at least 16,000 worth of calories per day in order to aid them in reaching the ideal weight meant to be considered beautiful. Fuller figures are considered ideal, and fattening the milk of the cow and camel are the sources to make their body go fuller. Since forcing women to be fed is not a good thing for them, the government has banned this practice.

Surgical Bandages
Nose jobs seem to be a very popular surgical work when it comes to beauty, but Iran is the country known as the capital for rhinoplasty. Not only are the women into this kind of business, but men, too. In every procedure, both men and women are always proud to put on those surgical bandages as a way of telling people that they have undergone the rhinoplasty surgery. This is also a sign to them in regard to social status and the path of ideal beauty. Which is why they wear the surgical bandages even after the wounds left by the surgery have already healed. Others who are not into rhinoplasty still think wearing the surgical tape is cool, so they wear it even if they have not undergone with the procedure.

Decorated Skin

Women do love to decorate their bodies with jewelry, but if you go to India, you will find women also decorate their skin with nose rings, henna and bindis. These are especially prominent when women there participate in certain celebrations and festivals such as weddings. The brides wear a "bindi", which is a red dot made from powder that is placed in the space between the eyes and above the nose, in order to look even more beautiful.

Straight Hair

Another highlight of Japanese women that makes them really attractive, even without that makeup is their straight stick hair. It is also considered as the most beautiful texture for a hair in Japan. Some of them have this natural hair, while the others that are born with wavy hair are very skillful in making them look straight. They use certain chemicals and even flat irons in keeping their as straight and sleek as possible. In many other countries straight hair is the standard of beauty as well.

Stretched Lips

Aside from stretched, long earlobes, here comes the stretched lips which is dominant amongst the women in the Mursi tribe, all the way from the southern part of Ethiopia. The women of this tribe insert the clay plates into the lower lips and will stretch them out. They incrementally increase the size of the plate in order to make their pouts bigger. This is a ritual considered to be a sign of sexual beauty and maturity.

Section 2: Simple Ways of Beauty Without Makeup

Another popular trend that mainstream and social media has lauded over the years is the use of makeup. Since a lot of video streaming channels feature women who are into teaching themselves how to try makeup by themselves, it has urged a lot of women to follow the same. They no longer need to go to makeup classes since there are people sharing their ideas for free online. However, women can achieve the epitome of beauty without adhering to the standards of society, and this is by not applying any makeup at all. This may sound absurd to those who have come to accept makeup as a way to make themselves pretty, but there are ways to look beautiful even without it.

Skincare

The basic foundation of beauty is skincare. When you prepare applying makeup especially when done by professionals, you will notice that they do something with the skin first before applying the makeup onto your skin. This is the cleansing method, which is not only applicable for applying makeup but should be done daily. If you live an urban life, exposing your skin daily to the industrial output of factories and many other machines, it is vitally important to cleanse your skin, especially on your face regularly in order to keep the skin looking very fresh. You should do this if you prefer to have a natural looking beauty rather than masking your face with makeup. Skincare is the most simple, easiest, and practical way to look beautiful.

Confidence

Women who wear makeup yet do not have any self-confidence will only ruin the makeup. People can easily sense women who are pretty and who aren't judging from the way they treat themselves, how they behave and how they smile. There are also women who feel that they don't look their best without makeup, which is why experts say it a lot that makeup should not be used as a mask to cover your real beauty but as a way for you to have fun with yourself. You should gain the confidence that you consider yourself beautiful without the application of makeup. If you continue believing that you are beautiful, others around you will start believing that too.

Grooming

One of the tips to keep your natural beauty is to make the most of the natural beauty you already have. There are different ways to approach, but take for example you have a kind of eyebrows that will need constant plucking, you must make sure that you keep this maintained at all times. As you take care of small details like that, you can make yourself look beautiful even without makeup on.

Smile

Make sure that your smile is as natural as you can make it. A genuine smile comes from a person with a genuine heart and those who are truly happy in the moment. People will quickly notice how beautiful a person you are rather than focus on the flaws you initially think they will notice.

Haircut

Did you know that changing your hairstyle from time to time will change the way you look at yourself? There are others that adorn hairstyles that changes how their faces look. Haircut will aid in making yourself look beautiful without the help of makeup. If you feel great and love the way your haircut is done, you will love yourself more. When you find a particular haircut that suits you, it will become your ideal beauty and you may no longer need any makeup at all. You don't have to hire the most expensive hairstylist, either. It is the skill that counts – find a recommendation from your friends or colleagues and you will get to the right style in no time.

Proper Sleep and Nutrition

The reason why many women in the workforce look very dull and unattractive even when they are wearing makeup is because they are not taking the proper balance of sleep and nutrition. They are focused too much on their work or taking care of their internal organs that they fail to realize that the skin is the largest organ of the body. As you take care of your inside, it will also show on the outside. In order to make your skin look beautiful without makeup, drink a lot of water and eat the right kind of food. You also need at least between 6 to 8 hours of sleep daily, too. This will help rejuvenate the skin from the stress built up in your body. As with balanced and healthy meals, you should look for a dietitian or nutritionist that will help you create a balanced menu with all the necessary vitamins to keep you healthy inside and outside.

Sunscreen

A lot of women ignore the heat and UV rays produced by the sun, which are two factors that will contribute to the early aging of the skin. You can maintain the youthfulness of the skin by applying sunscreen lotion to your skin on the face and the rest of your body before you make it out of your house. This is to protect your skin from the harmful rays of the sun. It will also help in aging your skin gracefully and not prematurely. It is also highly advisable to apply sunscreen when you swim and apply again for another two hours as the lotion is removed by constantly dipping into the water of the pool or sea.

Moisturizing Your Lips

This does not mean that you have to purchase the best lip moisturizer in the market. There is no need for lipsticks either. Your natural lip color is the best there is that matches up with your beauty. While the others have difficulty trying to look as natural as possible because their lip color can't be emphasized, what you need to do is to exfoliate your lips at least once every week in order to get rid of the dead skin. Moisturize your lips afterwards with a lip balm of your preference and you will notice a layer of skin come off the lips. Keep doing this in order to bring about the color of your lips without lipstick.

Exfoliating the Skin

You should not also ignore exfoliating the skin of your body and face. You should be doing this regularly in order to ensure the removal of dead and dry skin cells, leaving a glowing and clean skin. Remember to always moisturize your skin after exfoliation.

Other Natural and Simple Ways to Look Beautiful

1. If you are having problems with your hair looking dull, you should try the egg and banana hair treatment. This will help bring more shine to your hair. What you need to do is mix a mashed up banana and a single egg together. Apply the mixture to your hair and leave it on for between ten to thirty minutes. Wash the hair with how you usually do when you shower. For those who use conditioner bought from stores, you only need to condition the hair's ends after this treatment.

   Another way of conditioning your hair and make it look natural is by using a melted coconut oil and applying it to your hair. Some people use virgin coconut oil and apply it before they wash it away with shampoo. There is no need to apply for conditioner as the coconut oil serves as a conditioning for your hair. Make sure you leave the coconut oil for a number of hours. You can also apply the coconut oil before going to bed and wash it away at the next morning when you take your shower. A small amount of coconut oil on dry hair will also tame flyaway, stray hairs and add a glossy sheen.

2. There are also people who make use of the raw ingredients in the kitchen in order to make themselves look beautiful. One example is the Honey Facial mask, which makes use of raw honey as it has a natural antibacterial properties and is also a quick way in getting naturally soft and beautiful skin. Raw honey is to be applied to the skin at least once a week. Avoid the processed honey bought at stores. Warm the honey gently by using the friction of both your fingers together. Spread this on the face and leave it on for between five to ten minutes. Gently rinse your face off with warm water and pat it dry.

3. Avoid picking at your pimples or any other skin eruptions as it will leave black scars and spots on your skin.

4. Avoid the habit of chewing on your nails. Always have a nail trimmer ready and easily accessible so that you will no longer need to chew on your nails when the urge happens.

5   Don't rub your eyes too much or it will become infected. Some people have been reported to have damaged the cornea of their eyes because they exceedingly rubbed their eyes without knowing that a small particle has entered the area of their eyes.

6   Avoid drinking too much coffee or tea as it will dehydrate you and make your skin dull. It can also stain your teeth.

7   Brush your teeth at a maximum of two times per day and wait at least an hour after meals before brushing. If you brush your teeth after every meal you take, it will take off the essential enamel that your teeth needs. You can chew sugar-free gum after a meal to freshen your breath and also increase saliva which fights cavities.

8   Don't forget to maintain good posture when you walk, sit or stand idly. This will make you gain self-confidence and make you look tall and lean.

9   Avoid eating junk food excessively. If you feel you need to eat one or two, make sure that it is at a minimum and not taken daily. It is best to go with fresh vegetables, fruits, or any milk products and include them in your daily diet. However, it is best to keep your consumption at a minimum and make your daily meals into a variety.

10 Avoid drinking alcohol excessively. One glass may be enough, but it is best to avoid it entirely.

11 When you choose your clothes to wear for the day, aim for clothes that you feel comfortable and that suits you well. You should avoid wearing clothes that celebrities wear or following fashion trends that are not aimed for your body type. You need to understand the style that will fit you so that you won't feel awkward when you walk outside.

Section 3: Why Makeup May Not Equal Beauty

A lot of women today are very conscious of how they look, especially when they go outside. They spend a lot of time in front of the mirror beautifying themselves, only that they did not realize how there is only little impact that makeup can do to their overall appearance. As you are reading this, you will realize that things you have control, like smiling, will increase how attractive you can be to other people, even without makeup.

An example of this is how women will become more attractive if they tilt their heads a bit upwards. A lot of men find it very attractive with head tilting. The opposite is with how female look at male – they find it handsome when the men's heads are lowered a bit. Other factors include how people smell and their hormones. Hormones affect people's perception in a lot of ways. Women find various kinds of faces of male to be attractive at different stages during their menstrual cycle. Smell is equally important too.

Conclusion

Don't be disheartened when you find that makeup only makes up a little to increase your attractiveness to other people. If you are not comfortable without wearing makeup, you should continue doing so. However, keep in mind that what really matters is how you see yourself. Do you feel awkward or dejected when looking at yourself in the mirror? That is one indication that even if you wear makeup, there are people that will pickup on the way you look and treat yourself. What really matters is that you feel that you are beautiful and people will start to look at you that way. Stop using the mainstream media's standards of beauty as a way for you to achieve your standard of beauty. Going for the natural look and taking advantage of your natural features can often help you in becoming more beautiful for yourself and a happy, kind person is always a beautiful person.